A NOTE TO PARENTS

When your children are ready to "step into reading," giving them the right books is as crucial as giving them the right food to eat. **Step into Reading Books** present exciting stories and information reinforced with lively, colorful illustrations that make learning to read fun, satisfying, and worthwhile. They are priced so that acquiring an entire library of them is affordable. And they are beginning readers with a difference—they're written on five levels.

Early Step into Reading Books are designed for brand-new readers, with large type and only one or two lines of very simple text per page. **Step 1 Books** feature the same easy-to-read type as the Early Step into Reading Books, but with more words per page. **Step 2 Books** are both longer and slightly more difficult, while **Step 3 Books** introduce readers to paragraphs and fully developed plot lines. **Step 4 Books** offer exciting nonfiction for the increasingly independent reader.

The grade levels assigned to the five steps—preschool through kindergarten for the Early Books, preschool through grade 1 for Step 1, grades 1 through 3 for Step 2, grades 2 through 3 for Step 3, and grades 2 through 4 for Step 4—are intended only as guides. Some children move through all five steps very rapidly; others climb the steps over a period of several years. Either way, these books will help your child "step into reading" in style!

To Emelia Jane Gertner—L.R.P.

For Sam Pope—B.B.

The editors would like to thank DONALD BRUNING, Ph.D., Chairman and
Curator, Department of Ornithology for the Wildlife Conservation Society at
the Bronx Zoo, for his assistance in the preparation of this book.

www.randomhouse.com/kids

Library of Congress Cataloging-in-Publication Data
Penner, Lucille Recht.
Big birds / by Lucille Recht Penner ; illustrated by Bryn Barnard.
p. cm. — (Step into reading. Step 1)
SUMMARY: Describes the physical characteristics, eating habits, defense behavior,
and other aspects of large flightless birds both living and extinct, including
ostriches, emus, cassowaries, rheas, elephant birds, and moas.
ISBN 0-679-88968-X (trade) — ISBN 0-679-98968-4 (lib. bdg.)
1. Birds—Juvenile literature. [1. Ratites. 2. Birds. 3. Extinct animals.]
I. Barnard, Bryn, ill. II. Title. III. Series: Step into reading.
Step 1 book. QL676.P44 2000
598—dc21 98-51748

Printed in the United States of America   January 2000
10 9 8 7 6 5 4 3 2 1

Step into Reading®

BIG Birds

by Lucille Recht Penner
illustrated by Bryn Barnard

A Step 1 Book

Random House 🏠 New York

Most birds are small.

But some birds are
really, **really** big.

They are
bigger
than you!

The biggest birds
alive today are:

the ostrich,
the emu,
the cassowary,
and the rhea.

Can they fly?
No.

Big birds can't fly.
They are too heavy,
and their wings
are not strong enough.

Do they **ever**
use their wings?

Yes.
Rheas
spread them
to shade
their nests.

Ostriches
raise them
to attract
a mate.

The ostrich is
the biggest bird
in the world.

Its neck is longer
than a child.

Its eyes are
as big as
tennis balls!

Ostriches are fast.

They run faster
than people.

An ostrich can
even run faster
than a horse!

Ostriches can do tricks.

They can herd sheep.

Long ago,
Egyptians trained them
to pull carts.

Little birds **chirp.**

Not big birds.

They hiss, growl,

and rumble.

Emus make a
noise that
sounds like
a drum.

What pretty
feathers!

Rhea feathers
are fluffy.

Cassowary
feathers
are long
and thin.

People used to
put ostrich feathers
in their hats.

Big birds
swallow
strange things.

One ostrich
swallowed an
alarm clock!

A rhea ate
someone's money.
Hey!

Big birds fight
with their feet.
A cassowary
has super
sharp nails.

They are
sharp enough
to kill a man!

Wow!

Big birds lay big eggs.

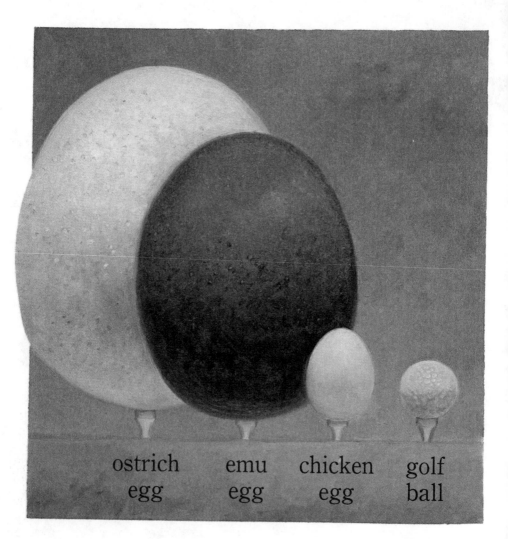

ostrich egg · emu egg · chicken egg · golf ball

A chicken egg makes
a meal for one person.

But an ostrich egg
feeds lots of kids.

Can you imagine
a bird as heavy as
a young elephant?

The elephant bird
weighed
1,000 pounds!

Its eggs were
bigger than
basketballs!

28

The moa was
the tallest bird
ever.
It was as tall
as two big men.
Moas and elephant birds
are extinct.
That means there are
no more
of them alive.

Who made
these footprints?
A big bird?
Or a dinosaur?

It's hard to tell.

Bird and dinosaur
footprints look alike.

Are birds related
to dinosaurs?

Many scientists think so.
What do **you** think?

FOR MORE
Information

Books

Colman, Penny. *Elizabeth Cady Stanton and Susan B. Anthony: A Friendship That Changed the World*. New York, NY: Henry Holt and Company, 2011.

Miller, Connie Colwell. *Elizabeth Cady Stanton: Women's Rights Pioneer*. Mankato, MN: Capstone Press, 2006.

Stone, Tanya Lee. *Elizabeth Leads the Way: Elizabeth Cady Stanton and the Right to Vote*. New York, NY: Henry Holt and Company, 2008.

Websites

Elizabeth Cady Stanton
www.history.com/topics/womens-history/elizabeth-cady-stanton
Find out more about the suffragist's life story and more about the women's movement.

Not for Ourselves Alone
www.pbs.org/stantonanthony/
Read about the partnership of Elizabeth Cady Stanton and Susan B. Anthony and their struggle for women's rights.

INDEX